PEARSON ALWAYS LEARNING

Danny Arnold • Ahmad Tootoonchi

Foundation and Practical Elements of Leadership

Pearson Learning Solutions, 501 Boylston Street, Suite 900,
Boston, MA 02116
A Pearson Education Company
www.pearsoned.com

Printed in the United States of America

1 2 3 4 5 6 7 8 9 10 V036 16 15 14 13 12 11

000200010270773392

MP

ISBN 10: 1-256-27617-0
ISBN 13: 978-1-256-27617-3

CONTENTS

PART 1: FUNDAMENTALS OF LEADERSHIP   1

PART 2: THE PERSONAL SIDE OF LEADERSHIP   9

PART 3: YOU AND YOUR FOLLOWERS   25

PART 4: RELATIONSHIP DIMENSIONS   37

PART 5: COMMUNICATION DIMENSIONS   53

PART 6: INFLUENCE AND MOTIVATION DIMENSIONS   59

PART 7: DECISION MAKING DIMENSIONS   67

PART 8: ORGANIZATIONAL DIMENSIONS   71

CONCLUSION   77

REFERENCES   79

COMMENTS   81

ABOUT THE AUTHORS

Danny R. Arnold

Dr. Danny R. Arnold is the Dean and Professor of Marketing in the Nelson Rusche College of Business Administration at Stephen F. Austin State University. He left the dean's position at Missouri State University to arrive at SFASU in August 2010. He was previously at Frostburg State University, where the major challenge involved obtaining initial accreditation from AACSB International. This goal was achieved in 2005. He spent the previous nine years as Dean at New Mexico State University and took the College on a successful journey to reaffirmation of accreditation. Before that, he spent fifteen years at Mississippi State University, serving the last five years as Associate Dean. He has spent a total of twenty-two years dealing with AACSB accreditation issues. He has published a number of books and textbooks, including 106 Leadership Tips, multiple editions of Business Strategy and Policy and of Strategy and Business Policy: Cases, Policy Expert, Effective Communication Skills, and Strategic Retail Management. He has also published over 200 articles, papers, and books. His articles have been published in journals such as the Journal of Business and Entrepreneurship, The CPA Journal, Entrepreneurship Theory and Practice, Journal of Media Planning, Journal of Personal Selling and Sales Management,

Journal of Business Research, Journal of Health Care Marketing, Journal of Commercial Bank Lending, Journal of Services Marketing, Personnel Administrator, Journal of Consumer Marketing, and the Journal of Professional Services Marketing. He has a new book entitled 147 Publishing Tips for Professors. He has also garnered a number of awards for his efforts and accomplishments. The awards were for teaching, research, and service activities. Dr. Arnold has been quite active in delivering contract research, consulting, and seminars.

Ahmad Tootoonchi

Dr. Ahmad Tootoonchi has a PhD in Leadership and Human Behavior. He joined Frostburg State University in 1989 and is now a Professor and Dean of the College of Business. He received the **Outstanding Faculty Award for Teaching** from College of Business in **1997** and from Frostburg State University in **1998** and **2003**. He has published numerous papers in various refereed publications and made several presentations at national and international conferences. He has also conducted numerous workshops/seminars for business, not-for-profit, and government organizations. He has been an active member in professional organizations, and received several Awards as Track Chair, Program Chair and Organizer of national and international conferences for Academy of Business Administration, Atlantic Marketing Association, and International Academy of Business Disciplines (IABD). He is particularly proud of his years of active involvement in IABD as Program Chair during 2003–2005, and now as President of this globally recognized institution (www.iabd.org). He also serves as the Chief Editor of the *Journal of International Business Disciplines*. More detailed information about JIBD can be obtained at www.jibd.org.

FOREWARNING!

If you have picked this book up expecting to find a panacea for transforming an individual into a great leader, *Stop*. You will not find it here.

If you have picked this book up expecting to find a new and novel approach for leadership, *Stop*. You will not find it here.

If you are looking for powerful ways to consolidate and wield personal power, *Stop*. You will not find much here.

If you are an experienced leader who might be interested in a review of some things that you do well along with some "food for thought," please proceed on to the Preface.

If you are a novice leader who is interested in some practical leadership tips that you can utilize tomorrow, please proceed on to the Preface.

PREFACE

This book presents and discusses some significant leadership elements which can help both aspiring and experienced leaders to lead their followers effectively, peacefully, and productively. The intent is that you will find strategies and tactics that you can use immediately in your work situation. You will find the book to be a "quick read," but we hope that some of the tips will cause you to have a "long think."

The overall focus is on developing positive leadership skills, and on avoiding those things that undermine good leadership. Consequently, you will also find both "do's" and "don't's."

Although the elements discussed in this book are geared primarily towards an organizational context, almost all are relevant for all types of leadership situations and positions. And, most of the suggestions are simply common sense.

As you read this book, remember that there are exceptions to everything—nothing is absolute when dealing with people. Further, there are no concrete formulas or magic panaceas for leadership. Solid leadership is derived from keen observation and hard work.

Everything presented here may not work for you. Pick those things that fit into your overall style.

Remember that, when you arrive at the managerial level, your survival depends upon your being a good manager. To truly *succeed*, however, you must survive, manage well, and develop *leadership* skills.

PART 1

FUNDAMENTALS
OF LEADERSHIP

A man in a hot air balloon realized he was lost.

He reduced altitude and spotted a woman below. He descended a bit more and shouted, "Excuse me, can you help me? I promised a friend I would meet him an hour ago, but I don't know where I am."

The woman below replied, "You are in a hot air balloon hovering approximately 30 feet above the ground. You are between 40 and 41 degrees north latitude and between 59 and 60 degrees west longitude."

"You must be an engineer," said the balloonist.

"I am," replied the woman. "How did you know?"

"Well," answered the balloonist, "everything you told me is technically correct, but I have no idea what to make of your information, and the fact is I am still lost. Frankly, you've not been much help so far."

The woman below responded, "You must be in management."

"I am," replied the balloonist, "but how did you know?"

"Well," said the woman, "you don't know where you are or where you are going. You have risen to where you are, due to a large quantity of hot air. You made a promise which you have no idea how to keep, and you expect people beneath you to solve your problems.

The fact is you are in exactly the same position you were in before we met, but now, somehow, it's my fault!"

Taken from: *www.jokesgalore.com*

No leader can achieve the pinnacle of success without possessing strong leadership fundamentals. To build the requisite strong leadership foundation you need to have a clear idea of your position, whom you intend to serve and lead, and why. You need to know where your organization is now, where you want to take it, and how. More importantly, you must believe deep within yourself that you cannot go through this journey alone—you need to work with your followers and help them find ways to work together in order for everyone to get to where you want to take them. Here are some tips that can help set the foundation of your leadership.

1. RECOGNIZE THE DIFFERENCE BETWEEN BEING A LEADER AND HOLDING A LEADERSHIP POSITION

You have likely known some good leaders. You have also probably known some poor leaders. Poor leaders are often individuals who have been thrust into leadership positions, but do not have the knowledge and skills they need to successfully lead people.

Holding a leadership position does not make one a leader— as having a driver's license does not make one a good driver, or having a child does not make one a good parent. Becoming a good driver, parent, or leader depends partially on an individual's personal characteristics and partially on some helpful knowledge and skills.

2. MANAGE FOR TODAY AND LEAD FOR TOMORROW

There must be a sense of immediacy regarding managing day-to-day activities. Most good leaders are also good managers. To be a good leader, however, you must focus yourself and your followers on the desired future and lead the organization to that future. You cannot let day-to-day minutiae cloud your vision of the future. Essentially, managers do things right, and leaders do the right thing.

3. STRIVE TO BECOME A SERVANT LEADER

Robert Greenleaf once said that great leaders view themselves as "servant first," and that this mentality is the key to leadership effectiveness. The first and most important goal of any leader is to serve the relevant group to the best of his or her ability—this approach provides the group with its best opportunity to achieve its goals. Becoming a servant leader is predicated on a genuine belief in that goal, and you must demonstrate it in your actions and interactions with others. This mentality can shape your followers' behavioral norms—good behavior is contagious! Servant leaders do so much for so many people so sincerely that it creates in others an equally sincere desire to imitate and reciprocate.

Contrast the servant leader to the individual who plays the role of "god/king" or "buck sergeant." This individual assumes the mantle of infallibility and omnipotence. Perhaps a few people in the world can make this approach work, but there are many approaches that work much better.

4. PROVIDE YOUR FOLLOWERS WITH HOPE

Great leaders find ways to provide hope to their followers and potential followers. Consequently, an aspiring leader should seek ways to boost hope. Leaders should evaluate the entire range of leadership tools and develop a set that fits the hope-centered concept. These tools will call for the leader to use words, actions, and attitudes to focus on building hope and optimism for a better future.

When a new individual assumes a position of leadership, many individuals (but not all) are naturally hopeful that the new leader will lead the group to a better situation. The new leader should focus on enriching this hope and avoiding things that reduce hope.

In general, generating hope involves painting a picture of the future that is better than the past and present situation. Show them that things are going to change for the better, and without great upheaval.

One of the authors once heard someone describe a "burning platform" approach. In order to get a group to follow the leader, the leader can either convince the group that (1) the present "platform" is burning and the group should follow the leader off the platform, or (2) there is a much better platform (future) to which the leader can guide them.

Another way to view hope-centered leadership from the leader's perspective is as follows:

1. Review the past and present,
2. share a vision for a better future, which should generate.....
3. hope, which should generate.....
4. motivation, which should lead to.....
5. action, which should lead to.....
6. group achievement.

5. CREATE A STAGE SO OTHERS CAN SHOW OFF

There is an old story told in the South about Bear Bryant. He was riding by campus late one night with a visitor who asked him about a light still being on in the athletics office. Bear's response was "That's just Joe _____ working to make me look like a genius." You must surround yourself with talented people who can get the job done. Then, you must create a situation in which your followers can excel and let them do it!

6. REMEMBER THAT THE JOURNEY IS MORE IMPORTANT THAN THE WAYPOINTS

Do not let specific events get you too high or low. Remember the old adage "This too shall pass." Leadership is a journey that contains peaks and valleys. Your objective should be to keep moving forward in a positive manner. Once you accomplish one objective, make sure you have others to pursue.

7. DO NOT EXPECT A PRIZE FOR GOOD LEADERSHIP

Many organizations have "manager of the year" programs. Do the criteria include leadership? Probably not! Such programs typically focus on short term accomplishments, which are the result of good management and not necessarily good leadership. Your rewards for good leadership are more likely to include personal satisfaction and subsequent promotions.

8. ARRANGE THINGS SO THAT PEOPLE WILL WORK TOGETHER

Ideally, leaders have followers who follow his or her lead and *work together to accomplish the relevant tasks.* It is up to you to arrange elements of the situation so that followers are able and willing to work together. You will likely never lead a group in which everyone likes everyone else. So, how can you encourage followers to work together?

- Create a vision (a master goal) that the whole group feels compelled to achieve.
- Establish specific objectives to support the master goal that involve your followers in work groups.
- Call occasional meetings for your followers to share the accomplishments of their work groups.
- Make sure your followers understand the interdependency between the accomplishments of different groups towards realization of the vision (master goal).
- Make sure your followers know that you are aware of individuals' contributions and that you value their team spirit.

9. IMPROVE PERFORMANCE BY CHANGING THE CULTURE

Improving your organization's performance may require changing the culture. Consider the following keys:

- To use a sports analogy, do you have "winning players" who have a winning attitude? If not, then your first step may involve changing the players. Essentially, you can accomplish this via subtraction, addition, and/or transformation:
  - Subtraction—terminate the "lost causes."
  - Addition—hire the right players.
  - Transformation—do things that cause people to improve; transform the situation and let people change themselves.

- Actions that can enhance transformation include:
  - Communicate your vision of acceptable, unacceptable, and exemplary employees (and their behavior).
  - Send signals of change. These signals can range from the subtle to the roof-rattling. One executive tells about his first staff meeting in a new management job. *I followed an unpopular manager who had a very different approach to leadership. At that first meeting, I walked into a conference room which contained a very large and long conference table. Everyone was sitting down the sides, with both end seats vacant. After greeting the group, I asked where my predecessor sat. Several pointed to one of the seats. I nodded and immediately strode to the other end of the table and took that seat. The group's body language was unbelievable! Most (those who understood the symbolic message) smiled and/or nodded approvingly. The message delivered—things would now be different!*
  - Promote the right people. Promotions based on seniority simply help cement the status quo. Promotions based on talent can send a powerful signal of change.
  - Change and/or clarify the evaluation process. People tend to respond to those elements on which they are measured.
  - Take advantage of storytelling opportunities. The stories you tell will illustrate the things you value and admire (or dislike!). A compelling story can actually create a "corporate legend." You must hone your storytelling skills!
  - Create a positive restlessness. People can sometimes get too comfortable and complacent. You do not want to "rule by fear," but you do want to communicate the need to "go forward."

PART 2

THE PERSONAL SIDE
OF LEADERSHIP

A fellow had just been hired as the new CEO of a large tech corporation. The CEO who was stepping down met with him privately and presented him with three numbered envelopes. "Open one of these if you run up against a problem you don't think you can solve," he said.

Things went along pretty smoothly, but six months later, sales took a downturn and the CEO was really catching a lot of heat. About at his wit's end, he remembered the envelopes. He went to his drawer and took out the first envelope. The message read, "Blame your predecessor."

The new CEO called a press conference and tactfully laid the blame at the feet of the previous CEO. Satisfied with his comments, the press—and Wall Street—responded positively, sales began to pick up and the problem was soon behind him.

About a year later, the company was again experiencing a slight dip in sales, combined with serious product problems. Having learned from his previous experience, the CEO quickly opened the second envelope. The message read, "Reorganize."

This he did, and the company quickly rebounded.

After several consecutive profitable quarters, the company once again fell on difficult times. The CEO went to his office, closed the door and opened the third envelope. The message said, "Prepare three envelopes."

Taken from: *www.jokesplace.com*

Before beginning to lead others you need to know who you are, what you have to offer, and to what extent you are able to work with and through people to achieve extraordinary goals. Further, you need to be truthful with yourself in terms of knowing your strengths, weaknesses, desires, needs, enthusiasm, commitment, loyalty, ability to handle conflicts, and your tolerance for stressful situations. The following are some helpful tips on how to handle the personal side of leadership.

10. KNOW YOURSELF

You can and should read and study the concept and application of leadership, thereby improving your leadership capabilities. You should also reflect on the leaders, both good and bad, that you have seen. What turned you off? What impressed you?

Remember, however, that everything you learn will not necessarily work for you. You simply cannot lead exactly like someone else leads. You must find new ideas, try them, continue to use those things that fit you, and discard the rest.

You must also remember that you have a learning curve —climb it as quickly as possible. In many leadership situations, you will be "treading new turf." There will be a lot to learn. If you are in a job situation that requires new skills, find out what they are and find a way to acquire them. This could involve, for example, furthering your education (formally or via self-study), finding a mentor or coach, or taking advantage of industry seminars and conferences.

11. FOCUS ON THE BIG PICTURE *AND* ON THE DETAILS

As a leader, you must be a visionary that can see the situation from 30,000 feet. You also must be competent with details. Inattention to details makes followers question your competence level.

12. COMMIT

You cannot do great things with a mediocre commitment. The primary difference between those who achieve great results and those who settle for a mediocre outcome is *commitment.* And, only 100 percent commitment is acceptable. If you are 99 percent committed, the probability that you will achieve some outcome other than excellence is 100 percent!

Committed people go far beyond the regular call of duty to achieve extraordinary goals, and as Koestenbaum said, leadership is about "commitment to greatness." Teachers who are not committed to teaching cannot expect their students to commit themselves to learning, and leaders who are not committed to great results, cannot expect their employees to be committed to high quality performance.

13. LEARN TO DEAL WITH COMPETING AND CONFLICTING DEMANDS

You, like every other leader, are caught "in between." No one has absolute power. Everyone answers to some one or some group(s). If you are in a leadership position, you have people above and below you. And, you are caught "in between," often having to deal with competing and conflicting demands and needs.

You are expected to be a good leader to your followers and a good follower to your boss, without sacrificing the satisfaction of one side for the sake of the other. The best approach is transparency and truthfulness with both sides. Never try to impose your own will on your followers by pretending that it is coming from higher up, and never try to ask your boss for more by pretending that you are being pressured by your followers, because the cloud will eventually clear up and every one will know the truth. In the face of difficulty and pressure, rely on your followers' creativity to find a solution, and manage the role-demands with honesty and integrity.

14. KNOW YOUR OWN RISK PATTERN

Great leaders develop an excellent sense for balancing risks and rewards. If you are conservative to an extreme, you will get nothing done. You will not be able to lead your followers to a better "state of being." Conversely, ignoring all risks will lead you to reckless behavior, thereby making it difficult to get others to follow you. Essentially, you need to do some good things while avoiding too many mistakes.

15. BE AWARE OF YOUR DECISION FILTERS

As a leader, you must make many decisions. Everyone possesses an array of information and decision filters. The information filters serve to place a certain value of various pieces of information. The decision filters establish rough criteria for your decisions. The critical message is that great leaders possess a balanced set of filters.

You have likely encountered individuals who possess unbalanced filters, or a single dominant filter. For some people, for example, the financial filter is dominant—every decision is a financial decision, regardless of the importance of other variables. For some, every decision is a political decision, perhaps to the detriment of the financial situation.

16. PAY ATTENTION TO YOUR PREDECESSOR'S STYLE

The style used by your predecessor and its results can have a great influence on which is the best approach for you to use. One executive tells of following a "dictatorial autocrat" who had destroyed the morale, motivation, and initiative of the entire organization. The approach he was successful with involved a heavy dose of "healing." He goes on to tell of his next position, in which he followed a world-class "nice guy" who provided very little guidance for the group. When our executive took over the organization, he adapted his approach more toward being an aggressive but caring leader.

17. DO NOT CRITICIZE YOUR PREDECESSOR

Although praise may not be warranted, you should refrain from criticizing your predecessor (directly or indirectly). He or she may certainly have enemies, but they may also have some strong supporters. Such criticism may unnecessarily aggravate these individuals. Besides, there is nothing to be gained by "tearing someone down."

18. BE ALERT TO DIFFERENCES IN THE PLANNING AND USE OF YOUR TIME

When you assume a new leadership position in a workplace situation, you likely achieved the promotion based on your expertise and hard work in your previous position. Now, you may be responsible for managing a much larger situation and your success may be predicated on the expertise and hard work of others. You must work differently. One executive tells of his experience when moving from a situation that was project- and detail-driven. His new situation called for leading and managing the big picture, while others handled the projects and details. He found that he no longer had much control of his calendar. And, the nature of his work day changed from a series of project-related accomplishments to one of meetings with both individuals and groups. He found this to be much more draining, thereby limiting the number of hours he was capable of working during a week. He also mentioned that it took several years for him to get comfortable with this new work pattern.

You must also guard your time carefully. Most jobs involve an array of minutia that are "time zappers." Without care, these time zappers can consume your entire day, thereby leaving very little time for the really important tasks.

19. DEMONSTRATE THAT YOU ARE WILLING TO WORK HARD

You cannot be a "casual leader" who is perceived as working at a minimal level. You must demonstrate that you are dedicated to getting the job done and are willing to work hard to do it. Essentially, you must lead by example.

20. DETERMINE WHETHER YOU NEED TO BE A MANAGER, ENTREPRENEUR, CHANGE AGENT, HEALER, OR SOMETHING ELSE

In some situations, you might be able to survive and lead effectively by simply being a good manager. Many situations, however, require you to be something more. The contingency management approach calls for you to assess the situation and determine the best style and approach to use. The situation, for example, may call for you to be entrepreneurial, such as by developing new products, programs, or processes. Or, you may need to be a change agent to transform everything ranging from attitudes to personnel. Or, you may need to take the role of "healer" if you find low morale and productivity.

21. SCOUR AND VET YOUR PERSONAL AGENDAS

So, you would love to push a certain project, perhaps just to prove a colleague wrong. That is a personal agenda. You want to launch a certain product because you are enthusiastic and optimistic, but your team does not share your optimism. Make sure your optimism is justified and that you are not pursuing a personal agenda. While a shared, compelling vision (agenda) for your organization can be a great motivator, followers generally can quickly distinguish between that and a personal agenda.

22. TRUST YOUR INSTINCTS

Yes, you must possess impeccable logic to be a good leader. Sometimes, however, logic can interfere with your instincts. An executive tells the following story. *I needed to hire a manager for a department that was not performing well. . . . I was desperate for a quick fix. After a round of interviews, my top choice turned the job down. My second choice took another position. I was left with the third choice. Since I was desperate, I followed my logic that dictated that I needed a manager NOW. And, I ignored the red flags being thrown up by my instincts—the red flags were indicating that this was not the right person for the job. Unfortunately, my instincts were cor-*

rect! I knew within a week that this individual was neither a good leader nor a good manager. I then admitted the mistake and terminated him shortly thereafter.

23. BEWARE OF YOUR PERSONAL NEEDS

Human needs can get in the way of good leadership. The human need for friendship can be particularly dangerous for a leader. Everyone certainly needs friends and confidants. Be very careful, however, about seeking friends within the ranks of your followers. Befriending a follower makes you (and the friend) vulnerable to criticism and can compromise your decision-making ability. Further, you should never make a leadership decision that reflects your need for friendship. Remember that you can be friendly with anyone, but can be friends with only a few. Look for friendship outside of your leadership role, including outside your organization.

You must also be aware of your need for power. All leaders must become adept at using power to influence followers in a positive manner. You have two major sources of power: position power (originating from your organizational authority) and personal power (originating from your character). You need to learn when, how, and to what extent you can use them effectively. You must keep in mind that your position power is limited by the authority vested in you by the organization, but your personal power has no limits and can be expanded and enriched as you grow as a leader through reflections and continuous learning.

The warning, however, involves your *need for power*. If the reason you want to be a leader involves the acquisition and wielding of power, then you may have a problem sustaining your leadership. The best leaders appear to want just enough power to get the job done. One executive shared the following parallel thought: *I was a young manager when people began talking about empowerment. I was not at all sure about the effectiveness of giving away power to employees. But, after much thought, I began to empower my workers. Much to my surprise, the more I empowered them, the more power they gave back to me!!*

There certainly are many other personal needs, such as the need for control, to be admired, and so on. The key is that not all personal needs can be met on the job.

24. AVOID BURNOUT BY CREATING AND GUARDING A SOUND LIFESTYLE

Do not let yourself become consumed with your job—you will burnout. Creating and guarding a sound lifestyle involves the following:

- *Leave your problems at work.* Regardless of how great your spouse is, he or she cannot solve your problems for you!
- *Concentrate on the positive.* Every leadership position involves some chaos and negative factors. Embrace the chaos and focus on the positive.
- *Take time to recharge.* Take real vacations and leave your electronic communication gadgets at home. If you cannot do this, you have not created other leaders to help you!
- *Put your family first.*
- *Establish outside pursuits.* Outside pursuits help you leave your problems at work. One executive tells about learning to play a musical instrument for the first time at fifty-five years old. He contends that the 30 minutes per day that he practices recharges his brain.
- *Have fun.* Have fun on the job and away from the job.

25. YOU WILL HAVE PSYCHOLOGICAL TROUGHS

No one can stay on a perpetual "high." You will not win every battle. You will face discouragement. Learn to recognize when you are psychologically "down." Learn how long your down cycles normally last. And, more importantly, learn how to shorten the down cycles and pull yourself back up to normalcy. Everyone has different tricks, ranging from long weekends to mowing the yard to fishing trips to playing with the grandkids.

26. MAINTAIN YOUR ENTHUSIASM FOR THE JOB

What is enthusiasm? It is a positive emotion that results from the excitement human beings feel about an activity or event. What is the opposite of enthusiasm—apathy and disinterest. Would you want to follow a leader who is apathetic and disinterested in the job?

True leaders feel excited and passionate about their job, which shows in their verbal and non-verbal communication. That is why true leaders can think of many good things that they can envision and do for their organization. They continuously think about something new and different that can help their followers feel more motivated and excited. If you do not feel enthusiastic about your work and your organization, it is time for you to reexamine your attitudes towards the profession you are in, and you will have to be as honest with yourself as one can possibly be. Try to determine the source of your lack of enthusiasm—is it you, the work environment, or both? When you find out the possible reasons, then you will have to take the necessary steps to deal with the situation constructively. This is extremely important, because if for any reason you lost your enthusiasm toward your work, your followers will soon lose their enthusiasm toward their work too, and the result could be a negative impact on the quality of work and life for you and your followers.

27. RESERVE TIME TO THINK

You may often find yourself neck-deep in alligators. Minute-to-minute and day-to-day demands can simply overwhelm. If you let the alligators consume all of your time, how can you take the 30,000 foot view (or soar with the eagles)? How can you think strategically? You absolutely must make the time!

28. DEVELOP A PROFESSIONAL AND PERSONAL CONFIDANT

You need someone to talk with—a confidant with whom you can share your problems and dreams. This individual may also serve as your mentor. This person may or may not be older, and may not be involved with your organization.

For many people, the spouse serves as a confidant. But, should your spouse serve as your professional confidant? For some, the answer is "yes." For most, however, the answer is "no." Most leaders should leave work at work, particularly personnel related matters. One executive says: *I will talk with my wife about things from work, but I never bring up anything negative regarding people. She actually prefers this approach and says "I do not want to know about people problems—that way, I can love everyone without regard to their specific work situation."*

29. TAKE CARE OF YOUR PROFESSIONAL DEVELOPMENT

The world is changing rapidly—knowledge is becoming obsolete at an increasingly astounding rate. You must keep learning and refreshing your skill and knowledge set to keep from becoming a dinosaur. For example, while you do not necessarily need to be the technological guru for your organization, a reasonable competence level can show that you are "with it." Never forget that you can also learn from your followers!

30. LEARN FROM YOUR SUCCESSES AS WELL AS FAILURES

You will experience success. Great leaders reflect back on their successful experiences and learn to utilize the contributing elements to generate future successes.

You will also make an occasional mistake. If you are doing *anything,* failure will occasionally raise its ugly head. First, get over it. Second, learn from the mistake and do not make the same mistake again.

Essentially, great leaders handle success and failure in the same way. First, they recognize that neither success nor failure is permanent. They do not rest on their laurels and they do not give up easily. Secondly, great leaders analyze the relevant factors for both success and failure. Unanalyzed failure has a nasty way of repeating itself. Unanalyzed success might make future success rather elusive.

31. KEEP YOUR AMBITION CORRALLED

Everyone possesses some ambition. Show only a little of it. Leaders who are publicly and blatantly ambitious can sometimes create distrust among followers. Have you ever heard statements such as "Well, he will not be with us very long—we can just do our jobs and ignore his exhortations" or "Every decision is made with her next promotion in mind"?

If your followers find out that you are conducting regular job searches, you may begin to lose their support. One executive shares the following: *Several years ago I was contacted by a head hunter about a "dream job." In my continuous effort to be open with everyone, I dropped a few casual comments about it. The story quickly made the rounds and the reaction stunned me. Some people were angry about my "disloyalty" while others simply became disinterested in anything I had to say. I did not take the job and it took me several months to recover. I learned a valuable lesson about keeping my ambition corralled.*

32. BE ABSOLUTELY TRUTHFUL AND AS OPEN AS YOU CAN

True leaders are absolutely truthful and as open as they can be in their personal and professional relationships. A leader must create an environment in which there is no perception of secrecy and secret deals behind closed doors. The leader's truthfulness and openness contribute to creation of culture of trust that results in a more cohesive and collaborative organization.

You need to practice openness. But, you must also practice being circumspect with information. This goes far beyond the confidential nature of certain information. Some information may not be confidential, but it may be something that you do not need to say. Examples include comments such as "Joe is thinking about transferring" and "Sue does not like Rachel."

You do not have to be so open that you share every piece of information with your followers. If you do so, you might cause information overload, which might make your followers feel overwhelmed with information that could be unnecessarily time consuming and negatively affect their performance. And, your followers might begin to ignore you and your communications.

33. KEEP YOUR EGO IN CHECK

Sure, you are bright, talented, and accomplished. If you have the right people around you, so are they. Remember that no one is infallible and no one is omnipotent. No one loves a leader who is "full of himself" or a "know-it-all." Humility and gratitude go a long way in attracting loyal, high performance followers.

34. PREPARE FOR EVERY FORESEEABLE OPPORTUNITY

Life is a story of endless opportunities. Great leaders have a sharp eye for seeing the opportunities and utilizing their own talents as well as the talents of their group members to take advantage of the opportunities. But, what you need to keep in mind is that you have to be prepared for taking advantage of opportunities, because if you are not, then in today's fast-paced competitive environment, someone else would beat you to it. Les Brown, a well known motivational speaker, once said, "It is better to be prepared and not have an opportunity than having an opportunity and not be prepared." Therefore, you must continuously keep yourself informed and maintain a high level of credibility, and be prepared for potential opportunities.

35. YOU WILL MAKE MISTAKES—ADMIT THEM AND RECOVER IN STYLE

Individuals with a traditional management mentality often have two negative characteristics: (1) they do not admit their mistakes, and (2) they try to pin the blame of their own mistake on others.

Unfortunately, there are still some people with this mentality in leadership positions in all kinds of organizations today. You must remember that individuals in leadership position live in a glass house—your followers are watching you. Your mistakes are most likely to be known by many, so your best approach is to admit the mistake, find out why things went wrong, determine how to prevent the same mistakes from happening again, and move on with pride on your side. Further, if you are the type of leader with a rich trusting relationship with others, your associates and followers can easily overlook your mistakes.

36. PRACTICE IMPECCABLE ETIQUETTE

A good leader should be an individual who can be admired by others from a number of perspectives. One of these perspectives involves good etiquette and manners. Crude and rude individuals do not generally attract many followers. Elements such as bad handshakes, poor table manners, poor greetings and introductions are definite "turnoffs." There are numerous books that can help you refine your manners.

PART 3

YOU AND YOUR
FOLLOWERS

*Two women were comparing notes on the difficulties of running
a small business.*

*"I started a new practice last year," the first one said. "I insist
that each of my employees take at least a week off every three
months."*

"Why in the world would you do that?" the other asked.

*She responded, "It's the best way I can learn which ones I
can do without."*

Taken from: *ajokeaday.com*

The success of leadership depends on three major factors:
the leader, the followers, and the situation. Throughout
the history, there have been many cases where a leader's failure was blamed on the complexity of the situation. In some of
those cases the blames could justifiably be placed on the situation, but in many others, the situational factors were used just

as excuses for failing leadership. In fact, it is in the face of difficulties and complicated situations that great leaders reveal their
effectiveness, because they understand their followers, believe
in them, empower them, inspire them, and make them believe
in themselves so the leader and the followers can work together
towards realization of the organizational vision. Here are some
tips on how to work with your followers effectively.

37. KNOW YOUR FOLLOWERS

Whatever your age, you are likely to have followers who
are both older and younger than you. You must take the time
to understand the general value systems of the different generations, particularly towards work and careers. The current
millennium or NeXt generation, for example, tends to focus
more on careers than on a specific job.

There are basically five types of followers.

- **Do-the-least followers:** The ones who do the least and
  always try to stay away from hard work.
- **Do-as-you-say followers:** The ones who do as you say
  without asking any questions or offering different ideas
  or alternatives.
- **Do-to-impress-you followers:** The ones who pick and
  choose to do only the tasks that might impress you, with
  an eye to ask you for a favor in return sometimes down
  the road. They do not do tasks for the sake of the group,
  but choose to do things to help themselves.
- **Aggressive-Negative followers:** The ones who always
  find something wrong about your initiatives. They always
  try to look for hidden motives behind every idea and/or
  action initiated by you and/or any other member of the
  group. Above all, they keep trying to influence the attitudes of other group members in an attempt to turn them

against you and your initiatives. They enjoy pointing out anything negative about you and the group, to people inside and outside the organization.

- **Authentic followers:** The type of followers that any leader should wish for. They give you their 100% effort, support, and honest perspective. You can count on their sincere support with or without your presence. They express their opinion and views for or against your agenda, but do it in a respectful and professional manner, and never make you look bad in the eyes of others.

How do you deal with each of those followers? First of all, you need to identify them through personal observation of their behavior focusing on characteristics explained above, and then handle them in the following fashion:

- **Do-the-least and Do-as-you-say followers:** Have them join your authentic followers, who can serve as role models and set a good example.

- **Do-to-impress-you followers:** Use their talent and good performance to the benefit of the organization, but be alert about the fact that they are expert in making you see them as an authentic follower. It is so important that you do not fall into this trap, because it might disappoint your authentic followers. You need to make a deliberate and determined effort to distinguish between the two and not to reward the do-to-impress-you followers the same as your authentic followers.

- **Aggressive-Negative followers:** Be absolutely open and transparent in your communication with your followers, which help reduce the credibility of whatever negative rumors an aggressive-negative follower tries to spread about you and your organization. If all else fails, terminate them—they drain the organization of positive energy!

• **Authentic followers:** They trust and respect your leadership, and certainly deserve your trust and respect. An occasional recognition and reward for their contribution is recommended.

38. YOU CANNOT BE A LEADER IF NO ONE IS FOLLOWING

To be a leader, you must arrange for other individuals to want to follow your lead. If you look around and no one is "behind you," then you are simply not leading. A counselor was heard to say "The person who thinks he leads, but has no followers, is only taking a walk!" Hopefully, mastering the tips in the book can help you attract followers in a variety of situations.

39. LEAD, FOLLOW, OR GET OUT OF THE WAY

A good leader knows how to lead, how to follow, and when to get out of the way. You need to know how and when to do each of the above. Since you cannot lead in every situation, know how to follow another leader. Sometimes, however, following may not be relevant—you may simply need to step aside and let others do the job.

40. YOUR LONG TERM SUCCESS IS PREDICATED ON IMPROVING THE QUALITY OF YOUR FOLLOWERS

On your last day on the job, what would you choose as the single most important evaluative criteria for judging your success? In many situations, if you have been able to improve the overall quality of your followers, you will have been successful. Most of the other issues will have been taken care of by good, talented followers.

41. CREATE A SENSE OF COMMUNITY

Human beings feel excited and find more joy in sharing stories and laughter with others in a social environment. This contributes to reduced stress and increased positive emotion. As it has been observed by sociologists, individuals do not express the same level of facial and vocal expression when they watch their favorite games on TV at home compared to watching the same game in a Sports Arena with a group of friends and thousands of other spectators.

In the workplace, leaders should engage their associates (followers) in various social events away from work and work environment in order to bring people together, and create a sense of community. In such environment, employees can feel more comfortable with each other and express their emotions more freely and openly, which could lead to higher morale in the workplace.

As Goleman (1995) indicated, everyone experiences both positive and negative emotions, but "in the calculus of the heart, it is the ratio of positive to negative emotions that determines the sense of well-being" (p. 57). Creating a sense of community among the followers can contribute to increased ratio of positive to negative emotions, which will lead to a psychologically healthier workplace.

42. DO NOT GIVE YOUR FOLLOWERS BLANK SHEETS OF PAPER

If you want your followers to develop something new and different from the norm, you must give them some idea of a direction. Giving a group an amorphous charge without parameters and expectations will generally lead to frustration and questionable results. One manager tells of giving a team the charge of developing a strategic plan. But he did not provide any guidance other than "do it." Surprise, surprise! It did not work!

43. TRAIN AND EMPOWER YOUR FOLLOWERS TO BE LEADERS

You will not likely be able to lead your organization relative to every issue that arises. Where does this leadership come from? You need it to come from your followers. Create and nurture leaders within the ranks—they can make you look like a hero! Creating leaders also provides you with an opportunity to choose your best role in situations: lead, follow, or get out of the way!

Great leaders understand that empowering followers does not mean giving up your power and authority. It is about developing your followers to a higher level of their potential so they can serve your organization in a more professional and effective way. Koestenbaum said that the right way of empowering people is to give them the autonomy to think and participate in decision making, provide them with a clear direction that is consistent with organizational goals, and give them sufficient organizational support. Keep in mind that you can be a more successful leader by surrounding yourself with better skilled and wiser people. You can accomplish this by empowering your followers to become more knowledgeable, better skilled, and wiser.

You need to optimize your follower's talents, including decision making. So, you must force decision-making on your followers. One executive describes his approach: *Every time I take a new position, I try to get people to take all the responsibility they can. One statement that I make frequently is "If I am gone for a month, I want things percolating so smoothly that no one will realize that I'm gone." Sometimes it takes people a while to grasp the meaning. Another statement I make often and early is "Either you can make this decision or I will make it—you make the call." Very seldom have I had anyone shirk the decision.*

44. DELEGATE. . . . DELEGATE. . . . DELEGATE

It can be helpful to distinguish between *assigning* and *delegating*. *Assigning* simply refers to assigning routine duties to someone else. This is a time-saver that prevents you from getting bogged down with routing minutiae. *Delegation* refers to giving someone else the responsibility and authority to make a decision or accomplish a task. Effective assigning and delegating frees you up for your real leadership efforts.

Micromanagers and bureaucrats simply "do the job." Leaders "get the job done." Do not try to do everything yourself—get help via delegation, constituency building, and empowerment. Conversely, do not over-delegate—people might think you are not doing anything.

45. ACCEPT THE FACT THAT SOME FOLLOWERS ARE ANTI-MANAGEMENT OR ANTI-YOU, REGARDLESS OF WHAT YOU DO

An old axiom states that about 10–20 percent of an organization will follow you because they respect you or your position, about 10–20 percent will oppose you, and the rest will "wait and see." You need to cultivate each of the groups in a positive manner. Do not let the "anti" get you down. While you should spend some time in an effort to transform their attitude, do not over do it.

46. DO NOT "VENT" AT FOLLOWERS OR ANY ONE ELSE

Yes, you may be the boss and feel like you can do anything you want to do. You might be able to get away with venting behavior for a while, such as allowing your frustration or anger at something to boil over in a follower's direction. But, remember that you really want to be a leader who has followers who are delighted to follow you. You do not want your followers withholding bad news and "walking around on egg shells." Venting takes away the delight and the followers.

47. DO NOT ALLOW INDIVIDUALS TO LAUNCH YOU AT THEIR ANTAGONISTS

It is common in work situations for a new leader (particularly from outside the group) to spend a great deal of time gathering and analyzing information, including about individuals. Some of this information about people comes from paper or electronic files, and some of it comes from other individuals. You must evaluate this information very, very carefully. You will frequently encounter negative relationships in which one individual will "tell you the dirt" on someone else (often in a very convincing manner). This individual's ulterior motive, which may be masked very well, could be to launch you at their enemy. Beware of the trap.

48. REMEMBER THAT THE ONLY PERSON'S BEHAVIOR THAT YOU CAN CONTROL IS YOUR OWN

You can lead people, but if you try to control their behavior you will not lead them for long. You can try to exercise leadership and influence to modify behavior. In the end, however, the only behavior you directly control is your own.

49. REMEMBER WHERE YOUR POWER AND AUTHORITY COMES FROM

To be a good leader, you must have power and authority to influence your followers. There are many types of power. A true leader's power comes from below—from the followers. Regardless of your "positional" power, you will not lead successfully unless your followers allow you to lead.

50. ACT ASSERTIVELY, NOT AGGRESSIVELY— CONFIDENTLY, NOT ARROGANTLY

Great leaders understand the difference between arrogance and confidence as well between aggressiveness and assertiveness. As a leader you must be able to walk the fine line of assertiveness. Assertive behavior is a desirable type of behavior, and is a reflection of a leader's ability to give constructive criticism in a polite and professional manner, and make others feel comfortable to behave in the same manner. Conversely, aggressive behavior is a reflection of one's selfishness and a desire to dominate others.

Further, great leaders are able to talk and behave confidently, but not arrogantly. Talking and acting confidently is a desirable attribute in a leader. You must, however, make sure to not put too much effort into sounding confident, as this can unintentionally push you toward the arrogance state. Followers are drawn to self-confident leaders. Potential followers distance themselves from arrogant people who hope to lead. Developing your leadership knowledge and skills helps an individual behave confidently.

51. EMBRACE DIVERSITY

Some of the best organizations are those that embrace and foster diversity. More diverse groups tend to generate more new ideas. Promote diversity regarding gender and multiple generations, cultures, and subcultures. Be sure to include a few radicals and rebels! A diverse group of talented people will often generate *positive friction,* which can be great!

52. FOCUS ON BOTH TASKS AND PEOPLE

Blake and Mouton developed a Managerial Grid that contains two dimensions: task orientation and people orientation. Based on these two 9-point dimensions, they identified different management styles: one that places the highest emphasis on task and the least emphasis on people (9,1), another one that puts the highest emphasis on people and the least emphasis on task (1,9). The third one is in the middle of the road with half emphasis on task and the other half on people (5,5), the fourth one does not really care about either task or people dimension of the job (1,1), the fifth one that seemed to be the most desirable places a high degree of emphasis on both task and people (9,9), which is called the TEAM style of management. The Team style is most desirable because an authentic leader understands that both tasks and people are equally important to the survival and success of the organization as well as the organization as a whole—without giving a careful attention and the support to your people, the organization's goal will not be achieved, and without accomplishing the organization's goals, the organization will not be able to survive in the long run. As a result, a good leader understands the interdependency between these two significant dimensions, which are crucial to the survival, let alone the success of the organization and the organization.

Overall, you must be good at handling both tasks and people. Some situations may call for you to focus almost exclusively on a task and other situations will call for a people orientation.

53. USE FOSA APPROACH FOR PROBLEM EMPLOYEES

Despite your best efforts, you will occasionally have to deal with followers who are not performing satisfactorily. An excellent approach consists of the FOSA acronym:

> *F = Fact.* Establish the facts of the situation, such as "You have been late seven times this month.
>
> *O = Objective.* State the desired objective or outcome, such as "You need to be on time every day."
>
> *S = Strategy.* Suggest one or more strategies for improvement, such as "You might consider getting up earlier or changing your morning routine." It might be even better to help the employee develop their own strategy!
>
> *A = Action.* Clarify the actions that will be taken if the objective is not achieved, such as "Your pay will be docked" or "You will be terminated."

If you have to take negative actions, your best defense in the court system is to have clear evidence that you followed a FOSA type approach. Using this approach can also be effective in changing the follower's behavior and keeping you out of court!

PART 4

RELATIONSHIP
DIMENSIONS

A businessman was feeling very ill and went to the doctor. The doctor examined him and backed away, saying, "I'm sorry to tell you this, but you have an advanced case of highly infectious rabies. You must have had it for some time. It will almost certainly be fatal."

"Could you give me a pen and paper?" said the businessman.

"Do you want to write your will?"

"No, I want to make a list of all the people I want to bite."

Taken from: *Jokes.Net Business Jokes: Buinessman Jokes*

It is obvious that this businessman did not have good relationships or relationship skills. Good leaders must be able to create solid relationships with followers and other people.

54. TREAT EVERYONE WITH RESPECT

"Respect cannot be demanded, it must be earned." Yes, you can earn a certain amount of respect by demonstrating a high level of knowledge, skills, and ability to get the job done. But, earning true respect is based largely on demonstrating respect for others. Respect is truly a "two-way street." Here are two corollaries:

- *Treat everyone with dignity.* Treating people with dignity creates followers. Ignore individuals' dignity and they will abandon you.
- *Assume the attitude that "everyone is valuable."* Even the worker who is paid minimum wage is making a valuable contribution—otherwise, why are you paying them?

55. BUILD POSITIVE RELATIONSHIPS

It is very common for people in a leadership position to pay a higher level of attention to their own group, department, or division. This could cause a negative long-term effect if the leader feels too busy and overlooks the importance of building positive relationships with others within the organization. People are, generally speaking, more helpful to those whom they know better and have good relationship with. Therefore, it is highly recommended that individuals in leadership positions take time out of their busy schedule to build positive relationships with colleagues in other parts of the organization.

You can build positive relationships with others outside your group by making an extra effort to participate in social events organized by your units/divisions. For instance, imagine in your organization, a division other than your own, is planning a retirement party for one of its long time employees, and is trying to generate more participation. In a situation such as this, you should make a determined effort to participate, even if it costs you money from your own pocket, because this would be considered an effort toward relationship-building with others. Generally speaking, human beings reciprocate good behavior, and as the old saying has it "it is in giving that you receive"; you take an extra step for others in a sincere manner, and sometime down the road, someone else will take an extra step to help you and your group. This is what servant leadership is all about!!!!!

56. ASK QUESTIONS, RATHER THAN QUESTIONING

One of the best ways to maintain good relations with followers involves "asking questions" rather than "questioning." Imagine, for example, that you are expecting an employee to give you a report before noon on today. It is around 11:30 a.m. and you have not heard from him. You pick up the phone to call him and inquire about the report. You may choose to inquire in one of the following ways. *Scenario one:* You might ask "where have you been; didn't I tell you that I needed that report this morning?" This is "questioning"— the language and tone of your statement reflects your lack of trust in his ability, in his work ethic, and in his sense of responsibility. *Scenario two:* You could say something like "Hi, how's the report going?" In the second scenario, the wording and the tone of your statement reflects your trust in his work ethic and his sense of professional responsibility, as well as your appreciation for what he is doing for you—but, it also gives him the message that he is about to be late with his report. This is called "asking questions" rather than "questioning."

57. BEWARE OF POLITICAL JOCKEYS

When you assume a new leadership position, you will establish new relationships with many different individuals. Most
of these people (hopefully) will be interested in a genuine
professional relationship. A few, however, will simply be trying to "feather their own nest" and have little real concern for
the organization or other individuals. It is critical that you dif-
ferentiate the political jockeys from those that are working
for the organization.

58. BEWARE OF ENERGY DRAINERS

Throughout the history, people have been classified in different groups in terms of their personality and behavior pat-
terns. One of the interesting ways was to group them as
energy drainers and *energy generators*. In your position as a
leader, you are likely to have both types in your organization, and must find ways to handle them. *Energy drainers* are
generally negative, make simple cases more complicated than
they actually are, and see a dark side in almost everything.
They have a strong tendency to complain about anything and
everything at home and at work. They might find a misspelled
word in your memo and complain about it for days to come.
In short, the negative and dissatisfactory nature of their comments and behavior tend to waste your group members' time,
thereby draining their energy. *Energy generators,* on the other
hand, are almost always positive, even when things go wrong.
In the face of difficulty, they seldom complain and, instead
of wasting the group members' time and energy with
complaints, they try to help searching for a constructive solution to the problem.

There are two helpful strategies for leaders to use in dealing with energy drainers. First, make sure to avoid hiring energy
drainers. Herb Kelleher, the co-founder of Southwest Airlines

once said, "We hire for character, and train for skills." You can do it too. Accomplish this by using personality tests available in the market, and/or by asking job candidates some open-ended questions based on work-related scenarios that can help you distinguish between potential energy drainers and energy generators. The human resource staff in your organization can help you come up with a few job related scenarios and relevant questions for use in the selection process. Second, try to get them involved in activities that require frequent contact with you, so you would be able to inject some fresh energy and enthusiasm in them; otherwise, they are likely to be ostracized by other employees, which will further escalate their negative attitudes towards the group and work environment.

59. TREAT EVERYONE FAIRLY

This is a "double-sided" tip. You must learn to treat followers that you dislike just like you treat everyone else. It can be more difficult for some potential leaders, however, to learn to treat people you like just as you treat everyone else. Your followers must trust you! Treating everyone with an "even hand" will garner respect.

A somewhat specific corollary is: *Do not make "back room" deals.* A "back room" deal with a follower can be viewed as a deal not offered to everyone and as one that you want kept confidential. Such deals are often viewed as unfair by others. This also can be viewed as another form of manipulation or even as an ethical issue.

60. LEARN TO WORK WITH PEOPLE YOU DO NOT LIKE

To be a good leader, you will have to learn how to work with superiors, peers, and followers that you do not necessarily

like. You must strive to keep your personal feelings from inter-
fering with your professional activities. People do not like to
follow a leader who is "controlled" by personal attitudes.

61. RESPECT OTHERS' OPINIONS, EVEN IF YOU DISAGREE

People like to be listened to! You must listen and respect others' opinions, even if you disagree with them. You can disagree as long as you do it tactfully and diplomatically—learn
to disagree without being disagreeable. One executive was
heard to respond to a comment in an open meeting "You may
be right but, at this time, I do not think that I can agree with
you." This comment actually diffused a tense meeting and
demonstrated that he had an open mind.

62. BE READY TO TAKE CRITICISM AND DISAGREEMENTS WITH GRACE

One of the most desirable characteristics in a leader is an
openness and confidence that enables the leader to receive
criticism with open arms and allow disagreements to be
expressed freely and openly. Your organization cannot
advance to a higher level of quality and productivity unless
you develop the ability to take disagreements and negative
criticism with grace. The worst possible reaction to criticism
is to become defensive, because:

- It will discourage your followers from coming to you
  with questions and/or criticism, which means you
  become less informed about your work environment.
  Colin Powel once said: "the moment your followers stop
  coming to you with their questions and concerns is the

end of your leadership, because it shows that they either lost their confidence in your ability to help, or they believe that you do not care. Either way, your leadership is finished."

- A leader who reacts defensively to criticism develops a tendency to blame others for his/her own mistakes, which will eventually lead to the demise of his/her units.

63. ACHIEVE THE REALITY *AND* THE PERCEPTION OF BEING FAIR AND ETHICAL

In this day and age, it is imperative that leaders conduct themselves in an ethical manner and strive for fairness in their dealings with others. This is a reality. Consider these questions every time you face a decision issue: "Is this decision fair and ethical? Will this decision be *perceived* as fair and ethical?" The reality and others' perception of reality are both important. Be sure with each decision that you would be comfortable explaining the decision on the nightly television news!

64. STAY IN YOUR SPHERE OF COMPETENCE

Depending upon your specific situation, your followers may possess a wide array of knowledge and skills. Do not try to "show off" your competence to someone who has superior skill. One firm had an owner who was loved and respected by his employees. One day, he visited a work site at which the employees were laying bricks for a patio area. Although he had never laid bricks, he insisted on helping workers for a few minutes. After he left, the workers had to remove all of those bricks because of the unevenness in that area. This owner strayed outside his sphere of competence and, for a while, lost a little of his luster.

65. SAVE YOUR AMMO FOR IMPORTANT BATTLES

You will occasionally have to "do battle" for an idea, program, or person. If all other avenues fail and the situation is important enough to go to battle, then you certainly want to achieve your objective. Remember, however, that there is always a cost associated with an outright battle—even if you win. If you are in a constant state of battle, you will likely lose the war—no one has enough ammunition for constant warfare. Conversely, if you "save your ammo" for really important issues, others will come to understand that if you are ready to battle, then the issue is critical.

66. LEARN TO MANAGE YOUR BOSS

If you work in a situation in which you have followers within a unit and one or more bosses, you must learn to manage your boss(es) to effectively lead your unit. No, we are not talking about manipulation and control. We are talking about managing your side of the relationship so that you have a reasonable opportunity to successfully lead your unit. Consider the following keys:

- You need to make an extra effort to understand your boss's views, philosophy, values, behavior norms, and sensitivity to various issues.
- A primary key to a successful relationship with your boss is effective communication. Learn, for example, what kind of case or argument has the best chance for success. One executive commented about one of his bosses: *I worked for a President who had many good traits. But, I had to learn how to bring new ideas, proposals, and problems to her attention. At first, I took the direct approach and failed miserably—she would reject every idea or solution. I finally learned that everything had to*

be introduced with an oblique approach. I had to carefully present pieces of a case so that she could generate the solution and claim it as her idea. This was a sad state of affairs, but I had to modify my preferred modus operandi in order to lead my unit effectively.

- Communication with your boss must be based on honesty, openness, respect, and trust. Your boss must trust you "to do what is right."

- Do not challenge your boss's authority at meetings or any other public gathering. If an issue of grave importance to you is being discussed at a meeting and you disagree with your boss, you must NOT allow your emotions to overshadow your professionalism. One approach (if it fits the situation) is to respectfully ask your boss if the decision-making can wait, so you can provide him/her with additional important information. Then, after the meeting, ask him or her for a private meeting, so you can express your persuasive disagreement and concerns to him/her in private.

- NEVER criticize your boss behind his or her back. It would be the worst thing you can do to damage your own reputation as well as the image of your boss and your group in the eyes of others, some of whom might enjoy listening to you and then spreading the words in an even more negative fashion.

67. DO NOT COMPLAIN ABOUT YOUR PROBLEMS OR OTHER PEOPLE

Chronic complainers and whiners simply cannot attract followers and, without followers, you cannot lead. Followers want to see someone who can solve their own and the follower's problems. How can you solve problems if all you do is sit around and complain about them?

68. REMEMBER THAT "YOUR WORD IS YOUR BOND"

This old homily is still around because it is still relevant. Essentially, if you make a promise or even a declarative statement (an implied promise), you have "given your word." You must fulfill any promise you make or your followers think you made. Consider this from a then new Dean of a business college. *I inherited a situation in which several faculty members had been denied a promotion and had appealed. The Vice President, rather than hearing the appeals, tabled the situation until the new Dean (me) could get involved. I held a meeting with each faculty member and his or her Department Head to get up to speed on their respective situations. During the meeting, I kept an upbeat attitude and promised each one that I would evaluate their situation carefully. Well, I overdid it! After deciding against the promotions and issuing the pertinent memo, I received a call from one of the faculty members who said that "I thought you said that you would support my application." I immediately backpedaled and said that I would call him back in a few minutes. I then called his Department Head and asked him if he thought that I had made that promise—he said "yes." I then called each Department Head and received the same answer. I realized that I had made an implied promise; I chose to stand by that promise. So, I called the VP and explained my rookie mistake. I also changed my recommendation to match the implied promise. I felt that standing by my word was more important in the long term than whether or not each individual was promoted.*

69. LEARN TO DEAL WITH CONFLICTS AND CONFRONTATIONS OBJECTIVELY

The best way to deal with confrontations is to arrange things so that no one ever sees a need for the confrontation.

Unfortunately, they will still arise and you will have to deal with them. Here are a few suggestions:

- Even if surprised, quickly determine your objective and do not lose sight of it.
- Define "winning." Your objective should not be to "win the confrontation." Rather, it should be to achieve an objective.
- De-personalize the situation. Leaving the problem-issue to float directly between two individuals can lead to personal attacks. Try to visualize putting the problem-issue "up against the wall" so that the two of you can get "shoulder to shoulder" and look at it objectively.
- Use a collaborating approach. Try to convince the other party that the best way to deal with the problem is working together, using creative thinking to come up with a constructive solution that results in full satisfaction for both sides. The significant advantages of this approach are: (a) it encourages people to work together, (b) it encourages creative thinking, (c) it depersonalizes the situation, and (d) it helps to reach a decision that brings full satisfaction to all involved. Keep in mind that collaborating is different from compromising, because in compromising, people do not have to work together, and the decision can lead to only partial satisfaction for both parties.

70. LEARN TO MEDIATE DISPUTES BETWEEN OTHERS

Even in a highly cohesive group, conflict and disputes can arise between two or more individuals, and it is all due to the fact that we perceive people and things differently based on our attitudes, personality, experiences, interests, and ambitions. Therefore, you must be able to mediate an occasional dispute between your followers. The most effective way to handle disputes involves anticipating potential conflicts and either arranging things so that conflicts do not occur or developing a process to handle them creatively. This means that you, as a leader, must know the attitudes, personalities, experiences, interests, and ambitions of your followers.

If a dispute erupts despite your best defusing efforts, then you should invite the disputing parties to a meeting at a time and place reasonably comfortable for both. If possible, provide some refreshments in order to make the atmosphere a little more informal. Ask each party to express his or her concerns and frustrations in a professional and non-personal manner, while you and the other party listen very carefully. Then, encourage them to collaborate to generate a solution that can lead to full satisfaction for both—it might not be easy, but it can work well in most situations.

So, what if the above "velvet glove" does not work? You might have to use a "hammer." One executive shares the following: *At a previous job, I inherited a good set of managers. But, I was warned that two of them had some serious personal animosity towards each other. Things went smoothly for several months. Then, the inevitable eruption occurred, and it was over something trivial. They began to zing each other in the meeting, which I stopped. Then, they continued the barrage via e-mail, including copying me. I felt that we were far past the velvet glove, so I called a meeting for the next morning. Once they arrived in the reception area, I invited them in and stated in a very calm voice, "Gentlemen, since this will take only a minute, you do not have to sit down. I have two things to say. First, I am very happy to have each of you as managers. Second, this zinging contest is over. My managers do not have zinging contests. You do not have to shake hands or hug, but it is over. Have a nice day." You could have knocked them over with a feather! They worked together effec-*

tively for seven more years and never had a cross word, even though they still did not like each other. The story of my handling of the incident also spread quickly and solidified my reputation of preferring the velvet glove while having the ability to deploy the hammer if necessary.

71. AVOID THE PERCEPTION OF MANIPULATION

Yes, you to have to arrange things to achieve short and long term goals. Followers typically accept this. Followers, however, do not like to feel that they are being manipulated. Manipulation is personal and generally viewed as Machiavellian or "sneaky." If you need someone's behavior to change, for example, take a direct and tactful approach rather than an oblique. Direct, unvarnished persuasion is not manipulation.

72. DO NOT LET THEM SEE YOU SWEAT

Yes, you may be in a competitive or "cutthroat" environment in which your would-be successors might love to see you squirm and fail. Fortunately, however, most followers really want to see their leader succeed. They want to feel good about the competence of their leader. You must therefore project the image that nothing makes you anxious or nervous. You want to project an image of stability and competence— developing a competent and stable character is the foundation for long-term successful leadership.

73. DO NOT LET THEM SEE YOU "BLOW UP"

This tip obviously deals with anger management. Let's consider the extremes, which you want to avoid. One extreme consists of the perpetually *angry person*. This individual always seems angry and demonstrates his or her anger at the least provocation. Such an individual will never attract followers. At the other extreme, we find the totally passive individual who never appears to be angry, regardless of the magnitude of the provocation. This individual who "shows no backbone" will also attract few followers. And, there are many gradations of anger in between the extremes. Good leaders are generally somewhere in the middle—slow to anger and "cool, calm, and collected."

Being angry and "cutting loose" is a different issue. *An obvious demonstration of anger control can be very impressive.* Blowing up can have disastrous consequences for a leader, particularly when you try to make decisions while angry. One executive shares the following: *I realize that I have the normal human reaction to stimuli—I get angry and frustrated similar to the average person. But, my followers think that I am very calm. I think one of the greatest reasons for this is my "72-hour cool off rule." When I get agitated at someone or something, I try my best to refrain from making any related decisions for 72 hours. This gives me time to conquer my emotions and, if necessary, gather additional information and/or perspectives. Then, I can deal with the individual or problem from a calm, rational perspective.* Never make a decision when experiencing any emotional extreme—either positive or negative!

Becoming angry is a perfectly natural human reaction to a frustrating situation, but how we react to an anger-producing situation is a reflection of our emotional stability and our ability to control our emotion under pressure. In other words, becoming angry is easy, but a leader must make sure that his or her anger (as Aristotle puts it) is "with the right person, for the right reason, at the right time, in the right way, and to the right degree."

While the 72-hour cool-off rule is great, do not forget the corollary: **Do not let problems fester.** If you have a problem (human or otherwise,) you must choose the proper time (and soon) to address it. Waiting too long will cause the problem to fester for both you and others.

74. IF YOU DO SHOW YOUR ANGER, MAKE IT MEMORABLE!

You want to demonstrate your ability to control your anger in frustrating situations, thereby becoming known as a leader with a high degree of emotional self-control. Occasionally, however, you can get away with showing your anger—if you are angry "with the right person, for the right reason, at the right time, in the right way, and to the right degree." When this occurs, *make it memorable!* Essentially, your show of anger can create an "organization legend" that makes the story telling rounds. One executive shares the following: *I worked for a division Vice President, who later became the company's President, for seven years. He was a world class gentleman who was very easy going and friendly. I saw him angry only one time in that seven years. A manager chose the wrong issue to push, and he did it in a very obnoxious and insulting manner. Since he ignored the warning signs such as a red face and throbbing temple, he was quite surprised when the VP finally went ballistic. Everyone else in the meeting felt that the VP was completely justified in his angry response. The story was retold many times and actually solidified the VP's reputation.*

Some feel that this tip embodies the Teddy Roosevelt approach: "Walk softly and carry a big stick." If you attempt to practice the humanistic tips contained in this volume, you will actually be walking softly. But, you also need to be ready to be tough and make tough decisions when called upon.

75. BE PREDICTABLE AND CONSISTENT

Consider the alternative—unpredictability. If you are unpredictable, your followers really do not know what you want from the organization or from them. Being predictable simply means that your followers know how you react to various situations and information. If you are predictable, they will be more comfortable talking with and sharing information with you.

PART 5

COMMUNICATION DIMENSIONS

An efficiency expert concluded his lecture with a note of caution. "You need to be careful about trying these techniques at home."

"Why?" asked somebody from the audience.

"I watched my wife's routine at dinner for years," the expert explained. "She made lots of trips between the refrigerator, stove, table and cabinets, often carrying a single item at a time.

One day I told her, 'Honey, why don't you try carrying several things at once?'

"Did it save time?" the guy in the audience asked.

"Actually, yes," replied the expert. "It used to take her 30 minutes to make dinner.

Now I do it in ten . . ."

Taken from: *www.jokesgalore.com*

Communication is simple—everyone knows how to communicate. . . . right? *NOT!!* Far too many people are poor communicators. This simple concept, however, has never been more important than it is today. Communication is arguably the single most significant key to leadership effectiveness, because no matter how exciting, attractive, and desirable a leader's vision, it cannot be realized unless it is articulated and communicated effectively to his/her followers. Further, ineffective communication can lead to misperception, misperception can lead to misjudgment of one's behavior, and misjudgment of one's behavior can lead to unnecessary conflict and tension in the work environment, which could lead to lower employee morale. Lower morale, can in turn negatively affect employees' performance and the overall organizational productivity.

76. LISTEN. . . . LISTEN. . . . LISTEN

Far too many people are poor listeners. A good leader is definitely a good listener. Further, a good leader is able to get people to talk so that he or she can listen. Many years ago, one of the authors had dinner with his boss and two wealthy business people. The boss demonstrated an amazing ability to ask questions. The other people left the dinner thinking that the boss was one of the smartest people they had ever met—all because he *asked questions and listened attentively!*

77. BE CAREFUL WITH OFFHAND COMMENTS

We tend to think of storytelling as consisting of "full-blown" stories. Simple statements, however, can be also be very powerful and have unintended consequences, particularly when taken out of context. One executive shares the following: *I was having a wide ranging, light conversation with another colleague over coffee. He described briefly a friend's situation that involved divorcing his spouse. I responded by mentioning a friend who married after high school; his wife worked and put him through undergraduate and graduate school—then he divorced her for a "trophy wife." Although I made no value judgments, the simple telling of the story was overheard by a junior executive. I later found out that he thought I hated him for his recent divorce, which I knew nothing about! Fortunately, word of his paranoia filtered back to me and I was able to talk with him and rectify the situation. It taught me a lesson!*

78. AVOID INTIMATE CONVERSATIONS AND BE CAREFUL IN TELLING JOKES

As a leader, you are not "one of the boys" anymore. Intimate conversations with followers, particularly of the opposite sex, can easily cause serious problems. Although you certainly need to have a sense of humor, be very careful with jokes, particularly off-color jokes. If you tell a joke, make sure that it helps rather than hinders your leadership situation.

79. LEARN TO BE BOTH TACTFUL AND DIRECT

Unfortunately, too many individuals are either tactful or direct, but not both. In dealing with your followers, you can be both. Being direct simply means being clear and not obtuse. Being tactful means that you choose your words carefully and deliver whatever the message is in a caring and considerate manner. So, be direct and tactful. It is truly high praise when followers consider you to be both diplomatic and a "straight shooter."

80. STRIVE TO BE OPEN-MINDED

Followers like leaders who have opinions and beliefs, but who are open to new information and ideas. One executive related the following story: *When I was a young executive, I got to know a senior executive who appeared to be a good leader and was a potential mentor for me. As our casual conversations began to take on more substance, I began to detect what I considered to be a fatal flaw. Neither I nor anyone else could have an open, free flowing discussion with him. He was very good at making you think he was open-minded, but all the time he was herding you towards his original position. It became quickly apparent to me that he was a decent manager, but had no followers due to this fatal flaw.*

81. STRIVE TO BE EASILY ACCESSIBLE

Authentic leaders are viewed by their followers as a source of support and someone they can count on when they need help. You must make yourself accessible to your followers, such as by visiting them at their work sites and by making other means of communications available to them (e.g., phone, e-mail). Most importantly, when they contact you with their questions and/or concerns, show them that you care through your verbal as well as nonverbal communication. The language you use in written communication, your tone of voice, your facial expressions, and your body language play a significant role in your followers' perception of you as a leader.

82. FIND A HELPFUL CASSANDRA (OR TWO)

The Cassandra Syndrome is a term applied to predictions of doom about the future that are not believed, but upon later reflection turn out to be correct. A Cassandra is obviously the person who makes the prediction. For a leader, a Cassandra is someone who is capable of providing you with "reflective, critical feedback." You need a Cassandra (or Devil's Advocate) you are comfortable with and who recognizes their Cassandra role and is comfortable with it and you. This reflective back-talk can help keep you grounded.

83. CONSIDER HOLDING "QUALMING" SESSIONS

Despite your group's best efforts, negative events can still occur, such as budget cuts, layoffs, strikes, natural catastrophes, and so on. These negative events create tension among everyone affected by them. You may want to consider holding a "qualming" session in which you allow people to express their reservations, doubts, and fears. You must also show them sincerely that you are in the same boat with them, and willing to do everything humanly possible to reduce the potentially painful experiences.

84. CONSIDER OCCASIONAL MEETINGS THAT FOCUS ON "WHAT ARE WE DOING THAT DOES NOT MAKE SENSE?"

Pet peeves get in the way of productivity. And, almost everyone has a pet peeve, often about something in the workplace that does not make sense. The more of these pet peeves you can eliminate, the smarter you will look.

PART 6

INFLUENCE AND MOTIVATION DIMENSIONS

"How long have you been working here?" one employee asked to another.

"Ever since the boss threatened to fire me."

Taken from: *ajokeaday.com*

Today, there are still managers who carry the traditional management mentality embodied by: "I don't intend to get into a popularity contest, I am here to do a job, and as long as I do my job, it does not matter to me if employees like or dislike me."

This phrase was valid for as long as managers focused on the day-to-day routine operations, and did not have to bother with the leadership aspect of their jobs. Today, any managerial position demands a transformation in the traditional management mentality. As Warren Bennis said "Managers are people who do things right and leaders are people who do the right thing." He summarized management as "activities of mastering routines" and leadership as "activities of vision and judgment." In today's competitive global environment, managers cannot choose to become one without the other—organizations need people who can be both managers of routine operations as well as leaders of "vision and judgment." That involves influencing and inspiring your followers, empowering them, and providing them with direction and support. However, you cannot truly influence, inspire, and motivate your followers if they do not like and respect you as a person, trust you as a leader, and believe in your ability to lead them to a better place. Now you might ask: should leaders go out of their way to do things just to be liked by their followers? Not really, but you will have to do simple but important things such as believe in and act with honesty and integrity, build trust in the hearts and minds of your followers, be concerned for their needs, and give them the recognition that they deserve. As a result, your followers will like, respect, and admire you as a person and a leader. Here are a few tips on how to enhance your chances for influencing and inspiring your followers in order to move them toward a desired direction.

85. BE A ROLE MODEL OF ETHICAL AND PERSONAL RESPONSIBILITY

In today's highly competitive global environment long term survival of all organizations depends on several key factors, one of which is commitment to ethical behavior. Ethics and personal responsibility go hand in hand. The principle of ethics holds that true leaders must think and act beyond their legal obligations and/or economic reasons to show that they care about "doing the right thing." What is the connection between being a role model and ethical and personal responsibility? Leadership is an act of influence more than anything else, and Vroom said that leadership influence has to be intentional and non-coercive. You as a leader must purposefully but non-forcefully influence your followers' attitudes and behaviors toward a more positive direction. Therefore, you must become a good example for your followers to look up to as a person committed to ethics and personal responsibility. Many individuals in leadership positions do not realize the extent to which they influence their employees' behavior by virtue of their own behavior, but it happens much more than they think.

86. INSPIRE THE TROOPS

A good leader inspires his or her followers. You should attempt to convert simple jobs and projects into *quests*. Ongoing inspiration for the members of the organization is as important as blood flow in the human body. What you need to remember is that human beings do not get excited and inspired by ordinary news, activities, or events. Consequently, you should be able to make your followers understand the connection between the smallest tasks to the larger vision (master goal) for the organization. You should be able to make your followers feel excited and inspired by reminding them that the projects they are involved in might be small in scope, but will eventually lead to a bigger and better outcome for the whole group.

87. CHEERLEAD AND PRAISE WHENEVER POSSIBLE

Good leaders must become adept at cheerleading and praising. One individual, for example, said that his greatest adjustment when assuming a president's position involved the much more frequent and greater need for delivering "attaboys."

Throughout his career, he had frequently been on the receiving end of praise. His adjustment was to the fact that he no longer received many attaboys and he had to become more adept at delivery. Praise can sometimes be just as important as monetary incentives.

88. CELEBRATE SUCCESS

All organizations have positive milestones or peaks. In addition to delivering appropriate praise, take the time to celebrate with those who helped achieve the milestone. Your specific situation will dictate "what are" and "what are not" appropriate forms of celebration. It can range from things like complimentary tickets to an event to a major celebration (e.g., banquet).

89. ENRICH YOUR EMOTIONAL BANK ACCOUNT WITH YOUR FOLLOWERS AND CO-WORKERS

Think about your regular bank account in which you deposit money regularly, and withdraw from it when the need arises. The more money you have in your bank account, the more secure you feel financially. Steven Covey says that you can open an emotional bank account in the heart and mind of people around you—instead of depositing money, you will deposit trust. You can deposit trust by being truthful, kind, supportive, and respectful to them, and by being there for them when they need your help. The kinder and the more truthful, supportive, and helpful you are to your followers the richer your emotional bank account. Then, they can more easily forgive you when you make a mistake or problems arise because you have built enough trust in your bank account to withdraw when needed.

You will likely have followers and a few truly *loyal followers*. Loyal followers are those that like and respect either you or the position; they will stand by you "in a pinch." You need to network inside your organization to expand your cadre of loyal supporters.

You will also need to become expert at networking outside your base organization. Relevant areas include areas throughout your larger organization, your organization's value chain, your community, and your profession.

90. REMEMBER THE THREE BASIC NEEDS OF YOUR EMPLOYEES

Sometimes individuals in leadership position are so occupied with their work responsibility that they forget that employees are humans with basic human needs. It might be helpful to remind yourself that your followers, like any other human beings have three basic needs:

- *Need to belong:* Human beings need to have the sense of belonging, such as to an organization, institution, club, and so on. A truthful, open-minded leader who treats his or her followers with respect and dignity is capable of creating a productive and cohesive environment to which employees can feel affiliated with pride.
- *Desire to learn:* Human beings have always had a desire to learn. They might not reveal this desire consciously, but they do feel this subconsciously. Good leaders make a deliberate effort to provide their followers with a variety of learning opportunities.
- *Desire to have something to offer.* All of us understand the negativity associated with the word "useless," and how good it feels to be useful. This phenomenon applies to all human beings across cultural, national, and racial

boundaries. Good leaders try to utilize all of their followers' skills and abilities in various ways, so everyone in the group can feel that he/she has something to offer to the organization, and is able to make a contribution to the growth of the organization.

91. HELP PEOPLE MOTIVATE THEMSELVES

Generally speaking, you cannot motivate people. You can, however, provide them with a goal, the support for achieving the goal, and a reasonable reward for achieving the goal. You should also find out what motivates your employees. You then can provide the means for your followers to motivate themselves.

92. RECOGNIZE TALENTS

It is unfortunate that many people in leadership positions take the talented members of their units for granted and in many cases treat them like any other employee. It is very important for you to identify the Talents in your organization and treat them the way they deserve. Here are a few important points for you remember:

- If you create a work environment with a non-caring culture based on "do the work, get the paycheck, go home, and leave the rest to us," the Talents will be the first ones who might think about leaving. Ordinary employees may be happy just to do the minimum and get the paycheck, but Talents work for more than the paycheck. Talents also are the ones who usually come up with new ideas and initiatives, so losing your Talents means, a big loss for your organization in the long run.

- Talented people do not like to be micromanaged, so you must give them sufficient autonomy to utilize their capabilities. A basic fact is that micromanagers are *NOT* leaders. True leaders draw out the best from their followers. Micromanagers provide potential followers with very little leeway in performing the job; rather, they simply have people do the job the way they want it done.
- Talented people often like to take a little risk relative to discovering new ideas and ways of doing things, so you must give them the freedom to take a little risk.
- Talented people need to establish relationship with you based on mutual respect, so you must show them the respect that they deserve.

To paraphrase a line from a country music hit song. . . . *Let the bosses run!* (it is actually referring to driving a pickup truck very fast). The point is that every organization has some thoroughbreds (the Talents). You need to identify them and create a situation in which they can forge ahead with enthusiasm and without artificial constraints.

93. ABANDON YOUR EGO TO THE TALENT OF OTHERS—TAKE ADVANTAGE OF YOUR FOLLOWERS' IDEAS AND CREATIVITY

Sure, you are smart and hard working—otherwise, you would not be where you are now. You should be proud of that! But, if you are leading a group of talented people, you probably cannot be better than they are at everything. Corral your ego and acknowledge the talent of your followers.

Regardless of how smart and creative you are, a collection of talented followers will generate more good ideas that you can alone, particularly related to their specific job duties. Take advantage of it!

94. IF A TASK CAN BE ACCOMPLISHED BY TWO PEOPLE, DO NOT ASSIGN FIVE TO THE TASK

Some individuals in leadership position assign tasks or projects to a number of their followers, without paying a careful attention to employees' individual characteristics in relation to the nature of the project. For instance, they assign five individuals to a project that could be accomplished by two or three people. By doing this, it might make some of your talented people feel that their time and energy were wasted or could have been utilized in a more productive ways. Therefore, in order to avoid wasting the time and energy of your productive followers, you must consider the nature of task and the number of people needed to accomplish it before assigning it to any of your followers.

PART 7

DECISION MAKING DIMENSIONS

The owner of a large factory decided to make a surprise visit and check up on his staff. Walking through the plant, he noticed a young man leaning lazily against a post.

"Just how much are you being paid a week?" said the owner angrily.

"Three hundred bucks," replied the young man.

Taking out a fold of bills from his wallet, the owner counted out $300, slapped the money into the boy's hands, and said "Here's a week's pay—now get out and don't come back!"

Turning to one of the supervisors, he said "How long has that lazy bum been working here anyway?"

"He doesn't work here," said the supervisor. "He was just here to deliver a pizza!"

Taken from: *Jokes.Net Business Jokes: Business Jokes*

Good leaders must make good decisions! The factory owner in the above story did not make a good decision. In fact, he violated many of the tips listed below.

95. CLARIFY DECISION MAKING MODES

The executive who shared this tip described his situation as dealing with bright, well educated research scientists. Group meetings in his organization were becoming bogged down with too much discussion (and bickering) and not enough decision making. After much thought and discussion, he and some colleagues formulated the following decision making modes:

    a. Your decision, you vote, majority rules.
    b. Your decision, consensus needed.
    c. My decision, but I need consensus.
    d. My decision, but I need your input.
    e. My decision, here it is.

Group leaders were trained to clarify to the group which of the modes would be operative for each decision issue. This approach is simple and it works!

96. CONCLUDE THE DECISION MAKING PROCESS WITH FIRMNESS

Regardless of the decision-making mode, at some point some one has to make a decision and this decision has to be clear and final. An executive shares his approach. *I try to make our decision making as open and collaborative as possible. I actually push everyone to provide input, even if it is counter to the "prevailing winds." I make it clear that dissension within the room prior to the final decision is encouraged. But, I also make it clear that once the decision is made, I expect 100 percent support—no "sandbagging" allowed! When talking with others, I tell them that the following type of attitude and statement is acceptable: "This decision was made. I disagreed with it, but I am fully supporting it." I have found this approach to be beneficial because it does not squash talent and, if the dissenter is correct, you may be honing talent.*

97. MAKE NO DECISION BEFORE IT'S TIME

Many people justifiably value the ability to make quick decisions, and you will feel the pressure to make them. You certainly need the ability to quickly analyze a situation, generate and evaluate potential solutions, and select the best alternative. Even if someone (e.g., for their convenience) is pressuring you to make a decision *now,* however, you should also give some thought to *when* the decision actually needs to be made. You will almost never have complete and accurate information. And, sometimes the *right* solution will not be immediately apparent. Consequently, you should determine exactly when a decision should be made—is it today, tomorrow, or 5 weeks from now? If the answer is today, then make the best decision you can make. You will sometimes benefit, however, by simply delaying the decision until it needs to be made.

98. EMPLOY THE FIVE Ws TO SIMPLIFY DECISION MAKING

Communication experts sometimes talk about the 5 Ws (there can be more): What, Who, When, Where, Why. You can use each of these questions (and others) to help frame a decision, such as:

- What—what is the decision to be made, what are the parameters, what are the consequences?
- Who—who should make this decision (me, someone else, a group)?

- When—when does the decision need to be made (now, tomorrow, next month)?
- Where—where does the additional information come from?
- Why—why does this decision need to be made, why is it important?

This overall approach will help you in delegating, managing your time, and ordering your priorities.

99. RECOGNIZE THAT THERE IS OFTEN MORE THAN ONE ACCEPTABLE ANSWER

Some individual's education, training, and experience have led them to believe that there is always one right answer. Not so! In many situations, there are several good and acceptable answers (decision alternatives, approaches). One answer may be better, but do you have the time and resources to find the absolute best answer (what is the cost/benefit of the effort)? Sometimes you obviously do have time and sometimes you do not. Choose a solution that you can defend and go forward.

100. REMEMBER THAT THE GREATEST ENEMY OF *GOOD* IS *PERFECT*

Yes, it would be great if every decision and every follower were perfect. *It's not going to happen!* Striving for perfection is a laudable goal. But, this very striving can sometimes cause progress to come to a grinding halt. Depending upon your particular situation, finding answers that are very good may be quite sufficient. If you are in a highly competitive and rapidly changing environment, your very survival may be predicated on finding some good answers quickly and going forward *now*. If you need your followers to think "outside the box," do not expect perfect solutions every time.

PART 8

ORGANIZATIONAL DIMENSIONS

The trouble with being punctual is that there is nobody there to appreciate it.

Taken from: http://www.coolbuddy.com/JOKES/

An organization is a system composed of four interrelated and interdependent elements: People, Structure, Goals, and the Environment in which it operates. The very existence and success of an organization depends on the proper alignment of every one of those elements. Everything else in an organization is either part of one of those elements, or is designed to support it. True leaders understand the importance of those elements and find ways to effectively and efficiently utilize them to benefit the organization as a whole. Here are some tips that can help you utilize the major elements in your organization.

101. CLARIFY THE ORGANIZATION'S MISSION, VISION, AND GOALS

You must determine whether the organization has a clear and useful mission, vision, and goals. If not, you must work to develop each element to provide direction for you and your followers. If you cannot articulate a clear and desirable direction for your organization, it is likely that no one will be interested in following you. Depending upon your specific situation, you may need to let people talk about and have input regarding the organization's vision and answer to the question "Who/What do we want to be?"

102. DETERMINE THE ORGANIZATION'S KEYS TO SUCCESS

Every organization faces a different environmental situation and possesses a different mission, vision, and goals. You must determine what it takes to be a successful organization in your specific situation. For example, the keys to success could involve acquiring advanced technology, hiring more and/or better researchers or salespeople, moving to a new location, changing certain processes, and so on. You might want to evaluate other similar organizations (benchmarking) to ascertain the characteristics of those that are most successful.

The benchmarking would help you to define for yourself and your followers the characteristics of a good organization, whether it is a corporation, a work group, or a volunteer committee for a club. You will then be able to answer a few important questions such as: What makes a good leader for such a group? What makes a good employee or follower for such a group? What should be the roles and responsibilities of the members of such a group?

103. DEVELOP A FEW MAJOR PRIORITIES

You cannot change everything overnight. Based on your analysis of the organization's keys to success, articulate and communicate those things that you expect to focus on. It may be as simple as "I will focus on acquiring new talent and my followers will focus on simplifying certain processes."

104. ANALYZE THE ORGANIZATION FROM A PERSPECTIVE SUCH AS THE "8 P's OF MANAGEMENT"

One of your first tasks is to get a grasp of the overall operations of the organization. One useful approach involves the "8 P's of Management:"

- *People:* Who are your followers? What is their experience, educational, and skill level? What are their needs and concerns?
- *Products/programs:* What output is being offered to whom?
- *Planning and Plans:* What planning processes are in place and what is the current and recent plan?
- *Policies and Procedures:* What are the rules and regulations?
- *Processes:* How do things actually get done?
- *Pennies:* What is the financial situation and prognostication?
- *PCs:* What is the technology situation?
- *Public relations:* What is the organization's image situation in the eyes of superiors, peers, and followers?

Understanding these elements will help make you a better manager.

105. TORPEDO THE STATUS QUO

You must make your followers understand that the status quo is absolutely unacceptable. Remember that old adage, "If you are not moving forward, then you are backing up." Acceptance of the status quo implies that the organization is doing acceptably well, which is unacceptable. One executive comments that in every job interview, he has made a statement something like "If you do not want changes, then take me to the airport!" Such an attitude helps to break down barriers to change and progress.

106. CONDUCT EFFICIENT MEETINGS

While conducting efficient meetings may appear to be a simple managerial task, it can also have great implications on your ability to lead. Unnecessarily long, boring meetings are discouraging and a waste of time. Effective meetings actually accomplish something. How many meetings have you attended that simply involved sharing mail and information (that could have been distributed in some other manner)? Remember the occasional meeting in which decisions were actually made? Make sure that your meetings are necessary and *focused on accomplishing one or more specific goals that need the participation of the attendees!*

Consider the following tips and cautions for conducting meetings:

- Very early, clarify the meeting's objectives, expected outcomes, rules of engagement, and the predominant decision making mode.
- Be careful with your own comments. Your statements and opinions can shift the direction of the discussion, which can be good or bad.

- Ensure that your comments are substantive. It takes only a few misguided or superfluous comments to create an atmosphere of "rabbit chasing," which is a waste of everyone's time.
- If you want people to listen attentively to your comments, do not talk all the time!
- Choose your battles carefully. It is okay to "cross swords" occasionally with another participant, but make sure the stakes are worthwhile and that your position is unassailable.
- Strive to be a questioner, clarifier, consolidator, summarizer, and concluder.
- Be sure to follow-up at the next meeting regarding any assignments from previous meetings, which will help solidify accountability.

CONCLUSION

Good leadership is predicated on an ongoing education process. People and circumstances continue to evolve, but the basic principles that allow you to deal with this evolution stay reasonably constant. Through the elements discussed in this volume, we have attempted to capture the essence of practical leadership.

Although leadership is a complex subject, one of the CEOs who previewed this volume feels that we have provided what amounts to a leadership checklist. He states that: *"Complacency will beget failure for those leaders that are not constantly following a well-designed checklist. Even though a pilot may have many years and many hours flying the same type aircraft, at the beginning of the fifth and last flight of the day, a checklist is completed in its entirety—the same attention is given to each item that was given to it for the day's very first flight.*

Hopefully, you have learned something new. And, hopefully, you will find the time to occasionally review these tips.

REFERENCES

Tip #2

Bennis, W. & Nanus, B. (1985). *Leaders: The Strategies for Taking Charge.* (pp. 21). New York: Harper & Row Publishers.

Tip #3

Greenleaf, R. (1977). *Servant Leadership: A Journey into the Nature of Legitimate Power and Greatness.* New Jersey: Paulist Press.

Tip #12

Koestenbaum, P. (1991). *Leadership: The Inner Side of Greatness.* San Francisco, CA: Jossey-Bass, Inc.

Tip #34

Freiberg, K. and Freiberg J. (1996). *NUTS! Southwest Airlines' Crazy Recipe for Business and Personal Success,* Austin, Texas: Bard Press.

Tip #37

Hughes, R. & Ginnett, R. & Curphy, G. (1999). *Leadership: Enhancing the Lessons of Experience.* United States: Irwin/McGraw-Hill.

Tip #41

Goleman, D. (1995). *Emotional Intelligence: Why it can matter more than IQ.* New York, NY: Bantam Books.

Tip #43
See the reference for Tip #12

Tip #50
Robbins, S. & Hunsaker, P. (2003). *Training in Interpersonal Skills: Tips for Managing People at Work*. New Jersey: Pearson Education, Inc.
Freiberg, K. and Freiberg J. (1996). *NUTS! Southwest Airlines' Crazy Recipe for Business and Personal Success*, Austin, Texas: Bard Press.

Tips #58
See the reference for Tip #34

Tip #62
See the reference for Tip #37

Tips #69 and 70:
Robbins, S. (1996). *Organizational Behavior: Concepts, Controversies, Applications*. New Jersey: Pearson Hall.

Tip #73
See the reference for Tip #41

Introduction to Part 6
See the reference for Tip #2

Tip #85
Vroom, V. (2003). Situational Factors in Leadership. In Chowdhury, *Organization 21 C* (pp. 69–87). New Jersey: Pearson Education, Inc.

Tip #89
Covey, S. (1989). *The 7 Habits of Highly Effective People*. (pp. 188–192). New York, NY: Simon & Schuster.

Tip #90
Chowdhury, S. (2003). *Organization 21 C*. (pp. 14). New Jersey: Pearson Education, Inc.

Tip #92
Kets de Vries, M.F.R. & Florent-Treacy, E. (2003). Global Leadership from A to Z. In Chowdhury, *Organization 21 C* (pp. 19–33). New Jersey: Pearson Education, Inc.

COMMENTS

- Each of our managers should read this book for a practical refresher about leadership!
  Susan Aldridge, President, University of Maryland University College
- A practical and quick read!
  Randall Bittinger, Chief Accountant for Allegany County School Board
- This is a great checklist, even for experienced leaders. Just like an experienced pilot goes over his or her checklist before every flight, good leaders should periodically review the fundamentals!
  Richard Hill, President, Rain and Snow
- A very useful, down-to-earth treatment of a very complex subject.
  Mitch Fralick, Partner, Producers Assistance Company
- I want all of my managers to read this!
  Sam Griffith, CEO, National Jet